KAISER CHIEFS

UNIVERSITY OF

With special thanks to the photographers
whose contribution of images made this book possible...

LUKE SEAGRAVE www.eFestivals.co.uk
CLARK WAINWRIGHT www.eFestivals.co.uk
STEVE GILLETT Live Photography

First published in Great Britain in 2006
by Artnik
341b Queenstown Road
London SW8 4LH
UK
Artnik is an imprint of Linveco AG

ISBN 1-905382-06-5

Design: Supriya Sahai
Cover and Design assistance: Marco Barbieri
Book Concept: Nicholas Artsrunik

Printed and bound in Croatia
by HG–Consulting

KAISER CHIEFS

Seamus Craic

artnik books

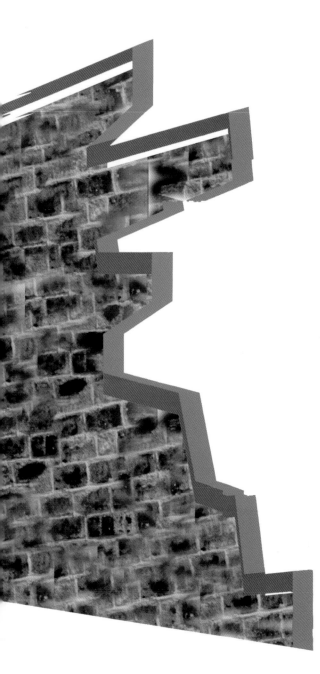

Introduction

Every so often a success story in music is a long time coming – a really long time. Somehow, the preferred pattern for bands themselves (and often audiences), consistent with the mythology of rock, is for a set of musicians to click instantly, start playing and build up an audience in no time, have a smash debut single, smash debut album etc etc. In short, to become 'overnight successes'.

Of course, it rarely happens, despite the mythology of rock. Even the story of the Beatles as told by some authors gives the impression that they were overnight successes, crashing into the charts in a sudden surge of Beatlemania – when they were, of course, languishing under the name of the Silver Beatles for a while, spent many dispiriting months playing a dingy club in Hamburg and the first single, 'Love Me Do', now a celebrated song the world over, was actually a minor hit of the day.

With the speed of communication these days, it may be that 'overnight successes' will become more the norm: witness the recent incredible success of a band like Sheffield's Arctic Monkeys, who have only been playing together for a very short time. In fact, they have only been actually playing their instruments for a very short time too.

Another band from Sheffield, Pulp, provide us with the antithesis to the overnight success myth. Pulp were a band who were well-known all over the city, a band that many indie fans in Sheffield had seen several times because they had been on the circuit for so long. Incredibly, they were originally formed in 1978, almost twenty years before they made any kind of breakthrough. When Jarvis Cocker was 'suddenly' discovered as the poet of college/bedsit land there were, to be sure, a lot of people in Sheffield who were having a wry laugh to themselves.

Sometimes looking back at a band's history, one finds that nothing really gets going while they are saddled with a name that just doesn't do them any favours. There's quite a few examples. Nothing really happened for Queen, for instance, while they laboured under the name of Humpy Bong. Similarly, Faith No More were originally called Sharp Young Men and struggled Pulp-like with them name (and for the record, Pulp were originally called Arabacus Pulp in their early days).

One of the biggest bands in the UK at the moment also carried the weight of a Bad Band Name. It was like they had had bad karma but once a new name was decided on, things started to happen.

Who would have thought that the Kaiser Chiefs were once known as Runston Parva?

Runston and Parva

The road to the Kaiser Chiefs via Runston Parva is a long and winding one, involving some disparate characters indeed. The main character is a man called Ricky Wilson – not that that is his original name either. Born Charles Shirley Richard Marjorie Wilson in1978 in Leeds, he changed his name to Ricky when he was still young because he thought it sounded 'cooler'.

He attended Leeds Grammar School and early on developed an interest in the arts, no doubt influenced by his father who worked for the BBC. A shame then (not to say a tragedy) that his father is the executive responsible for *It's A Royal Knockout*: featuring the two most contemptible members of the Royal Family by far (Prince Edward and Sarah Ferguson) and a host of stars (Meatloaf, John Travolta, John Cleese) who should have known better, it was a PR disaster – as well as appalling TV – bearing as much relation to the arts, in fact, as the Royals do to everyday family life.

A mere nine years old when this happened, it at least gave Ricky a good sense of what was not cool.

A couple of years later, across town, three boys aged eleven met at their new secondary school: Simon Rix, Nick Baines and Nick Hodgson. Simon and Nick Hodgson soon came to know the other Nick as 'Peanut', a nickname that was a hangover from his previous school:

'We had to draw a picture of ourselves when we were about 10 and I drew this picture and my head looked like a peanut. I threw it away and drew another one but someone found it in the bin and for the last 16 years I've been called Peanut!'

The three of them started to hang round together and all developed a keen interest in music at the same time. From the age of fifteen they were playing music together with various bands: Simon played bass, Nick played drums and Peanut played keyboards. Being so close it was probably inevitable that they would one day form a band together, but they were still missing a complimentary member or two and they carried playing gigs and checking out the vibrant Leeds club scene with more than half an eye out for suitable cohorts.

The other members that emerged from the shadows of the clubs couldn't have been more different. Guitarist Andrew White was slightly less music-obsessed than the trio that he ran into at a club one night as he was a highly successful student, known as 'The Dux' at school for his academic prowess; he was also a great cyclist and a Yorkshire BMX champion. What he had that impressed Simon, Nick and Peanut was a certain quietness, a sense of right-on gravitas that they didn't have (exemplified by his dedicated vegetarianism), nicely combined with a sharp sense of humour.

Presumably, a sense of humour was there, but gravitas nowhere to be seen when they first clapped eyes on Ricky – playing with a Rolling Stones tribute band. They saw someone who was quite different from Andy, a restless ball of energy on stage, someone who had all the makings of a great frontman for the band.

This was at the Cockpit club, in the Swinegate area of Leeds on the 'Brighton Beach' night. The Cockpit was one of the most popular clubs in Leeds and has hosted in its time bands like Placebo, the White Stripes, the Hives and many more – in fact, it was a hive for the indie scene. Ricky was asked to join the band after introductions were made. He was reluctant at first, mainly because he had now graduated from art school and a career may have awaited him as a lecturer but, as he mulled it over, he and Nick set about, with the other's help, getting another night together at a different club with a different sort of vibe.

Setting up at the Hi-Fi club, they inaugurated 'Pigs'. Pigs was essentially an electro-punk bash, which pulled in an assortment of mainly style-obsessed indie kids who weren't, however, indie purists – like the five members of this nascent band. Simon later said of the music element: 'We set it up because there were no club nights in Leeds that we wanted to go to anymore – there were all sorts of indie nights that weren't good. It's an indie disco but we play more kind of new wave and a lot of things you don't get elsewhere.'

Meanwhile Ricky, ever the arbiter of cool, saw it also as something of a fashion statement: 'We just wanted somewhere we could go where you could wear a top hat and no one would beat you up. I used to be in the little patio outside my house with spray-cans, coloured paper and ribbons, doing the posters. And everyone would take 'em home. I'm like Andy Warhol on a very small basis. My patio was The Factory.'

It was a night that became legendary with tales of stage invasions, widespread drunkenness and debauchery, and a particularly memorable night where the bouncers banned Nick from finishing a night with Motorhead's 'Ace Of Spades' because it was bound to cause just too much aggro.

And music from the likes of Motorhead would stand happily alongside 'Vienna' by Ultravox or 'Teenage Kicks' by the Undertones, while Ricky and Nick's increasingly minimalist posters would attract more and more punters intrigued with the arbitrary inclusion of phrases like 'Tits' and 'I Am Gay'.

The club scene was in the foreground of their lives perhaps at this point as Ricky took his time accepting the offer of a place in the band – the fact that at the time, as Nick laughingly recalled later, that 'we didn't have any songs!' may have had something to do with it. In 1997, though, the band finally came together and set about writing some songs and thinking of a name, though Nick and Simon decided to go off to university (to return later) and the band without a name consisted of Ricky, Peanut and Andy.

They looked to their own backgrounds for the inspiration for the band name and in the tradition of the Bay City Rollers and Chicago, they chose a place name for themselves. Choosing the distinctly un-showbiz sounding Runston Parva after an anonymous little village in the Yorkshire Wolds near to Leeds.

To the villagers it would have sounded like they were trying to make the name even more downbeat by adding an *n*, because it is actually Ruston Parva, and they had all got the name of the place wrong!

Even more incongruously, the music they started playing was not, say, the grinding rock of a band like Manchester's the Fall or the northern 'hymns' of the Verve – Runston Parva decided to play garage rock. They had their first practice at Mainline rehearsal studio in Leeds in January 1997, played their first gig in the summer at the Duchess in Leeds, and played their final gig in, at Joseph's Well in Leeds. They barely made it out of their hometown because they were, in fact, pretty diabolical.

Of course, a lot of musicians would have guessed that they weren't any good because garage rock is about as simple and raw as rock'n'roll gets, being music based on simple chord progressions, pounding drum and short, repetitive lyrics. The essence of a good garage band is strong songs and good timekeeping – Runston Parva had neither and it was back to the drawing board as Simon and Nick came back from university.

It was also back to the daily grind for all of them while they struggled to determine how to move forward with the band. Ricky had still maintained his art studies and was now doing an art lecturing stint for a couple of days a week at the Leeds College of Art and Design – as well as the obligatory 'shitty jobs'.

Andy did 'shitty jobs' most of the time while Nick split his time between DJ'ing and being a nutritionist. Peanut worked in a bar, and Simon was his boss!

They worked on their musicianship, having been inspired (in what was perhaps another classic piece of poor timing) by the Britpop bands. This was 2000, and the Britpop era was probably at its height three or four years earlier when they were just starting the band, but for all of them it was the determining influence on them: Nick has called it 'the best thing that happened in British music for the last 20 years.'

In 2000, though, there were few people who would have agreed with such an assessment. The heady Nineties days of the Blur v. Oasis rivalry, echoing that of the Beatles and the Stones in the Sixties, and Jarvis Cocker humiliating Michael Jackson seemed long gone: a truncated Oasis didn't seem capable of coming out with another great album, Blur and Pulp were showing signs of wear and tear and there were a host of bands like Menswear who were dumped by their labels.

For the Leeds quintet, Britpop still resonated and they resented somewhat the new wave of American music that was starting to make inroads into the British scene. Peanut put it this way, looking back on it later: 'We were all teenagers when the Britpop thing happened and then, while The Strokes and the White Stripes were good, there was suddenly a wave of dross from America that we're all, in our own way, reacting against.'

Though they still weren't quite good enough to escape from the garage rock format, which, ironically, was a predominantly American genre they did see that they had to make their home identity, their Britishness part of the band's image and appeal.

They reconvened with a new name: Parva.

This seemed like a throwback to Britpop too where all the bands seemed to have one-word names: Blur, Oasis, Pulp, Placebo, etc.

Though they were galvanised by this new direction and were sadly very hopeful, this was an era which is, if anything less fondly remembered than the Runston Parva era by the band: Peanut has said, 'We were younger and easily influenced by everything. We made every mistake you could possibly make.'

They played relentlessly and even managed to get some money together, with their perilous incomes, to get some recorded output – and it sank without a trace. They had two years struggling along, these Britpop anachronisms, as US bands dominated the UK indie scene. They managed to get a record deal with Mantra only for the singles to sink again without a trace of royalties and, before their album could be released, Mantra folded, leaving Parva high and dry. All their work was being ignored everywhere.

They tried to break into London but only found the same dismissive attitude to them that they were finding in Leeds in the band's lowest point by far. Peanut said, 'I think there was a mass murmur in London saying

"Hey, let's not go anywhere near Parva".'

If anything it was actually even worse in their hometown, where some of their rivals found their plight hilarious. Peanut has tried to blot it out it seems: 'We were really skint and I was quite depressed at the time. There's lots about that period that I don't remember.' Nick was quite the opposite: 'We were very low and I had to keep the morale of the troops up. We had a lot to prove to ourselves. It wasn't just to prove it to ourselves, it's because you're making huge claims about what you're going to achieve in life in front of everyone and if you don't actually do it, it means you're a failure, aren't you? I do get some satisfaction from thinking there are certain people who are really annoyed by our success.'

At the time, though, they were back in their shitty jobs and while Ricky, for instance, might have been gaining a living lecturing, he had to make ends meet by setting up other bands in a club, some of whom were enjoying the demise of Parva; all of whom were getting much more of an audience than they had ever got.

It was time to go back to the drawing board once more and get rid of Runston and Parva.

The third era of the band found them again looking homewards for inspiration to find the new band name. Rather than going out into the Yorkshire Wolds, they chose to stay closer to home. All of the band members were keen football fans and dedicated fans of Leeds Utd: 'We love Leeds United,' said Ricky later. 'We don't go every week – well Simon and Andy do whenever we're not recording or touring – but we do follow them through thick and thin.'

Using this as a source of the name seems as incongruous as choosing the name of a nondescript village in Yorkshire and providing echoes of Britpop. Like Britpop, Leeds had just said goodbye to a golden era. After unprecedented levels of investment in the club, a team filled with a few (highly paid) stars had reached the dizzy heights of a Champions League semi-final. But this was soon followed by a collapse in their fortunes: relegation, an acrimonious sacking of the manager, the team falling apart and the stars whose huge salaries had virtually bankrupted the club taking off like the proverbial rats on a sinking ship.

Lucas Radebe, the club's celebrated defender, was one star who had chosen not to leave and he was a firm favourite among all the Leeds fans. The South African-born Radebe was also one of his home country's sporting heroes, captaining the national side and part the most celebrated football team in South Africa – Johannesburg's Kaiser Chiefs.

Once this name was suggested, it was pretty much a foregone conclusion. Where Runston Parva or Parva were neutral if not weak names, Kaiser Chiefs conjured up associations of strength and power. They also knew that if they built up a fanbase, they would be called 'The Kaisers' – which is what has happened. But whether The Kaisers or Kaiser Chiefs, it was an inspired idea.

It may have been fun choosing the new name but a lot of midnight oil was burnt on what had to be done to turn round their fortunes. They all had a shared vision of playing triumphantly in front of their home crowd at the celebrated Leeds Festival, but it had become uncomfortable clear to them that for this to happen they would have to raise the standard of their musicianship and the quality of their songlist. Along with changing their name, they decided that would work harder at their instruments, dump all their old songs and write new ones.

With this radical new approach to everything, they had a new revelation:

'It was like seeing the light,' said Ricky. 'We'd been trying so hard to fit in that we'd lost sight of what we were best at – not fitting in.'

What this meant in effect was, once again, being true to themselves and being a northern band, relating to all the realities of northern life. Ricky 'stopped singing about working on a railroad and going to high school proms and starting writing about being broke in Leeds' Hyde Park.'

The days of the garage band were over.

The Kaisers

To a certain extent, the indie days were over, too. More often than not the indie scene in the UK has always had a peculiar vein of evangelism running through it, not only on the part of the artists and the indie press but even some of the fans.

As the scene grew out of the punk movement, it had adopted some of the sense of being on a crusade against mainstream music, espoused by the likes of the Smiths, Echo & The Bunnymen and, later, the Stone Roses. Very rarely it seemed, was humour allowed in: it was either deeply subtle, as in Morrissey's lyrics, or deeply unsubtle like, for instance, Shaun Ryder – not that the Happy Mondays ever gave the impression that they were on any crusade.

Moreover, as the circulation of the indie press started to go down year after year, every new indie success was trumpeted more vehemently and in more depth than it had been before. The **NME** was keen to prove when **Melody Maker** closed down that they had their finger right on the pulse, otherwise the tabloids and broad-sheets, which were giving in-depth coverage to indie music, would kill the old rock bible too.

As the Kaiser Chiefs were coming into being, the latest indie sensation were a band called Franz Ferdinand. This was a band that tipped its hat to the NYC model of punk rather than the Britain's insurrectionary Summer of '76. Their sound had strong echoes of Talking Heads and Television: cerebral music that connected with the youth not so much because of what the band was saying, but because they were perceived to be cool. Franz was a highly talented band that was also popular with their peers; nevertheless there is a frigid quality to them, which was mirrored in all their coverage. Virtually all of it over-earnest and po-faced.

Coming at people with a name like Parva, the Kaisers realised that they had been pretty over-earnest about it themselves. Looking back at these pivotal moments in the **Independent On Sunday**, the band totally agreed with the assessment that they 'knew that they had to leave behind everything associated with Parva. They had put six years of effort into being indie cool and got little in return.'

So, now, it was Ground Zero.

'We had no songs, no name and no money,' Ricky remembered. 'It was the most exciting day of our lives.'

Peanut added: 'Whatever anybody tells you or wants you to believe, nobody wants to sell no records.'

This wasn't an embrace of the mainstream, but more a real sense that they hadn't been true to their own ambitions nor themselves and Peanut has provided a series of dazzling quotes to illustrate this: 'We used to write songs for ourselves and, if anyone else liked them, it was a bonus. Now we write songs for other people and, if we like them, it's a bonus... we write lyrics to please ourselves and, if anybody else hates them, it's a bonus.'

It was a high wire act that they were attempting. They were on the same 'crusade' of indie believers but were looking to conquer Mammon not the Holy Land.

As the quotes show, the Kaisers weren't without humour (Andy White is generally considered the quietest of the band, for instance, but all of the other members of the band credit him with being the funniest by far). Ricky says: 'We're funny people and we spend most of our time trying to make each other laugh, so it's only natural we should try to get that across in our music.'

In the new era of meaningful rock, they felt they just couldn't afford to be po-faced about anything. As they turned their minds to the new songs that they needed to produce, they knew they had a rich store of humour and pathos in the lives that they led and observed.

They may root it in Leeds but they soon found that they could tell stories in their songs that had universal appeal. Songs that featured too many drinks one night, National Express coaches or fumbling and flirting with girls – it was, if you like, Little Britain music.

And this was the other high wire act that they had to bring off – how to lack seriousness while still being taken seriously.

They also took a look at what they were wearing and rejected any kind of brand identity:

Their 'look' was a mishmash of styles, faintly reflecting the ska revival that occurred when they were born, but that was mainly because of Ricky and his penchant for pork pie hats.

In general, it was a case of everyone wearing what they felt most comfortable with – and it was a world away from the look of Franz Ferdinand which had a Television/Kraftwerk vibe. The Kaisers started off banning jeans from the band; at their first Kaiser Chiefs gig, Ricky wore a tracksuit and flat cap. He said: 'Some of the early experiments with what we wore were stupid. The thing that made it was when we put a hat on Peanut's head.'

What's the difference between Parva and Kaiser Chiefs? Peanut's got a hat on.

The band closeted themselves away before coming out live with the new songs, which were definitely more catchy – none of this indie anthem rubbish – but this was all planned as well... 'Most of them were written as audience-pleasers so when everyone left the night they'd say, "Weren't Kaiser Chiefs good?",' Ricky said later. And lo and behold, they found that they had the kind of reception that they had been waiting for all those years with songs they had come up with (intended for the debut album) in less than six months.

They quickly developed an enthusiastic live fanbase and, all of a sudden, the A&R men were out and about having been tipped off about a band called Kaiser Chiefs – and some of them thought they looked strangely familiar. Of course, many of these people knew all about Parva and the unreleased album and had spread it around that the band were 'has-beens': this was also part of an increasingly ageist attitude that the Kaisers had long noticed in A&R men. Ricky explains:

'A&R men see human ages as dog years – if you're past 25, you're dead.'

And this led to the Kaisers being very coy about their ages until only recently, as the word got back to them that they were 'too old' – despite their all being in their mid-twenties. It was a worrying thought, especially if you thought of a band like Ash or, even worse, Supergrass, who were then releasing for 2004 their **Supergrass Are 10** retrospective – they were the same age as the Kaisers!

Undaunted, the band took careful note of the reception that they were getting. They knew that they were pleasing people and it was worth risking some money on another single to see if they could get any serious label interest from it. They got in touch with indie label DrownedInSound who agreed to release a single for them if they recorded it. They chose one of their most infectious tunes, 'Oh My God', which they recorded in Nick's bedroom

Time on your side that will never end
The most beautiful thing you can ever spend
But you work in a shirt with your nametag on it
Drifting apart like a plate tectonic
It don't matter to me
It's all I wanted to be

'Oh My God' was like the polar opposite to the lean angular and sculptural sounds that Franz Ferdinand were producing.

The Scottish band were restrained, and even uptight on their most tuneful songs and there was always a real sense that they weren't able to 'let rip'. Meanwhile, 'Oh My God' is three minutes and thirty six seconds of instantly danceable music, comprising a cunningly catchy piano part in the intro, an echoing riff that reverberates in your mind long after and a vocal delivery that glories in Ricky's Northern vowels. On top of that was a blinding chorus of foot-tapping delight – it was the perfect debut single for the Kaiser Chiefs.

In the event, DrownedInSound were choked that they only pressed the limited edition single that came out in May 2004 because it sold out in a week in the few outlets that carried it.

Incredibly, it even got to No 66 in the charts.

It was the splash that they had been waiting for years – and this time, the irony of ironies, the A&R men came with chequebooks and there was a line-up people wanting to sign them up.

They managed to hammer out a deal with B Unique records, an indie label, under the umbrella of Polydor and Universal in the US.

After eight years of struggle, they were about to start recording another single, next an album was being scheduled... After so many years of trying to get people interested in them, they had finally been recognised as worthy of being promoted properly. It was still hard to believe and Ricky was soon to say: 'The pressure has gone completely. If you'd looked at us in our rehearsal room two-and-a-half years ago, when we hadn't played anything for two hours and we'd just been talking about what the hell are we going to do, and everyone leaves fucking miserable, when you know that's happened and you look at us now how could there be pressure?'

emerge presents...

Kaiser Chiefs
El Mocambo
feb. 15th 05
Toronto

For one thing, they had done such an astute deal that there was no pressure from anyone at the label even to enhance their image – which apart from the die-hards most of their fans conceded could do with a bit more polish.

They were emerging not only as the ice-cool Franz Ferdinand were dominant but also at a time when Pete Doherty, the dissolute Libertines/Babyshambles frontman, was bewitching the rock'n'rollers looking for a rebel who'd frighten their parents.

Anyone going behind the scenes with the Kaisers would soon see that they were no rock'n'roll wildmen.

Ricky, for one, was now gaining quite a reputation as a front man of unparalleled intensity.

The rollerball style of performing that had been seen in the Cockpit in Leeds was still there and he would leap around stage and tear into all the songs with abandon, stunning audiences with his unselfconscious swagger. The irony was, of course, that he was a bag of nerves.

He had always been a sickly child and would throw up before every gig, suffering from 'intestinal migraine'.' This is something that he has only just conquered, but recently, Ricky – one of the UK's most assured live performers – has suffered an ectopic heartbeat on the road and has had to cut both dairy and caffeine from his diet.

Peanut suffers from an irrational fear of sharks, with the emphasis on irrational: as Andy said once – 'it's amazing to see a grown man so scared of something he has only ever seen on the television.' What could have been most damning of all was the large collection of soft toys that the Kaisers take on the tour bus with them.

But they were disarmingly honest about their idiosyncrasies and Peanut's response to questions about their life on the road was, well, unintentionally hilarious: 'I have to have my hat, and because you tend to get a bit ill on tour you've got to have things like water and fruit every day – so we try and keep healthy and look after ourselves. And at the moment I'm doing something for Radio 1 about healthy living on the road, so we've got a reporter following me and Ricky round asking us how we feel all the time.'

Somehow, though, they were getting away with it. And it was all just beginning.

'I Predict A Riot'

The next single was already decided on: not only was it a classic, it was also irrefutable proof that this definitely wasn't a band of wankers. Ricky looked back on his days as a DJ in the clubs in Leeds and provided a devastating snapshot of northern life full of latent aggression: 'I used to DJ at this indie club in Leeds and would have to drive past this horrible mainstream club where everybody was pissed and police vans were packing people in.'

The almost child-like wording of the song at the beginning

'Watching the people get lairy
Is not very pretty I tell thee
Walking through town is quite scary
And not very sensible either'

seems very gauche at first, especially the use of a word like 'thee'. In reality, it sets the scene perfectly for the rest of the song's contents, featuring chip fat, beatings and condom-buying girls, all of which conveys the cultural wasteland that such images spring from. The child-like diction reinforces the sense of the inevitable and the feeling of normality, which if you think about the lyrics can induce a numbing pathos.

Even more jarring is the matter-of-fact warning of the chorus:.

I predict a riot, I predict a riot
I predict a riot, I predict a riot

It was a song encased in the kind of muscular power pop arrangement that the Jam specialised in. Live audiences had already taken it to their hearts and the single version had retained the incendiary power of the live version – as well as showcasing the incredible melody. The single went to No 22 in the charts and this time, the press were raving about them. There were a lot of comparisons with the Clash's epochal single 'White Riot' and if they had been part of a wider movement the comparison might have stood up.

But the Kaisers, or the Chiefs as they were also being called, were their own movement and things were certainly moving now... UP.

The most important result of the coverage was that they were singled out by the **NME** to open the **NME** Awards Tour 2005 in February. This was a coveted slot in the music calendar, already well known for sealing the success of both Franz Ferdinand and Coldplay when they were given the chance to do it. Those may be the more successful bands ultimately, but the Kaisers made more of a searing impression than either of those bands did, as the breathless report from the **NME** showed: 'Taking to the stage to a huge roar, the Chiefs waste no time in whipping the crowd into a frenzy.

'Lead singer Ricky Wilson is a flying blur as he careers around the stage, seemingly only one step away from madness.

'It's hard to believe this is the same band that supported the Ordinary Boys at the Waterfront last autumn. Their biggest single to date, 'I Predict A Riot', nearly lifts the roof off the place as bodies fly around. This shouldn't be happening. It's 7.30pm.'

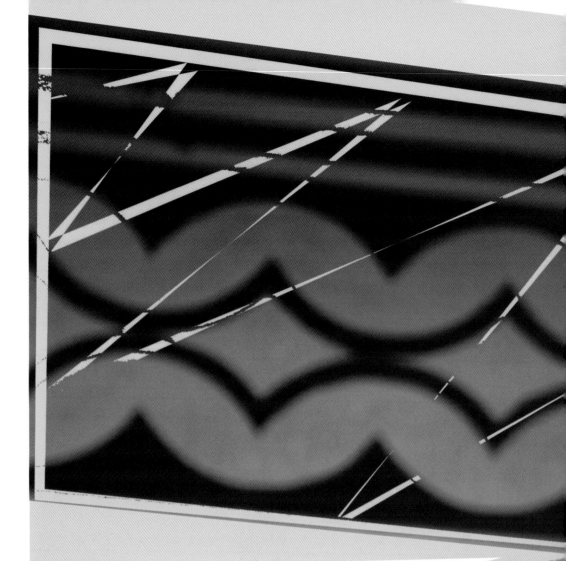

It was a out-an-out triumph for the band and the perfect scene-setter for the album that was due in March.

They had been in the studio for some weeks and they were privileged enough to be working with one of UK indie music's most celebrated producers.

Stephen Street had actually contacted the Kaisers about producing their album and the honour wasn't lost on them: not only did they know him as the producer of the Cranberries and XTC, he was the producer of indie icons, the Smiths (and Morrissey) and Britpop icons Blur.

Blur were another important influence on the Kaisers, encouraging the 'art pop' element of the band.

Just as Blur had brilliantly evoked their London locale in **Parklife**, the Kaisers wanted to do the same with their debut, expressing what it was like to be living and working (or not working) in a northern town, having laughs and/or feeling low.

Street was the perfect foil for this: he was the sort of producer who would become closely involved with all aspects of an album, not just getting the band to run through the songs, but also conceptualising with them and even (as in Morrissey's solo albums) co-composing. With Blur, he was instrumental in helping create a masterpiece and many of the band's fans charted the band's decline from when he was no longer involved – even Graham Coxon had returned to work with him for his acclaimed solo album, **Happiness Is Magazines**.

For the Kaisers, he was ideal but what's more, once they began working together, he became an even greater fan of the band. This was encapsulated in one tribute to the band's lyrics that Simon recalls: 'He loved the line "birds of a feather and you can be the fat one", which I laugh at.

'I think that line's completely silly, but Stephen Street thought it was one of the best lyrics he'd ever heard... And he's worked with Morrissey!'

Once together, Street and the Kaisers turned to their concept and they came up with the idea of simply calling the album , **Employment**.

Where **Parklife** suggested London Town shot though with various pleasures, **Employment** is a grim and witty evocation.

In the post-industrial north, where job security has become a thing of the past in an economically depressed area, words like 'employment' and 'jobs' hang over people and even haunt them, affecting relationships and preventing people from enjoying life to the full.

The Kaisers wanted to suggest that life could be enjoyed, adding humour to the kitchen sink realities that they were describing in song. Nowhere was this articulated better than in the forthcoming single, 'Every Day I Love You Less and Less' with its tale of a guy who's so over his ex-girlfriend that he feels obliged to tell her how great his life is without her (which is his displaced was of telling her that he's pining): it's a man who shrouds his feelings in humour, tries (not very hard) to be magnanimous but can't help being hurtful in the end.

Lyrical Work

'Impressed you're dressed to SOS
Oh, and my parents love me
Oh, and my girlfriend loves me
Everyday I love you less and less
I can't believe once you and me did sex
It makes me sick to think of you undressed
Since everyday I love you less and less.'

And it's also there in 'Born To Be A Dancer', where Ricky
summons up the image of a kitchen sink anti-hero whose mind
is constantly elsewhere, in work and life in general – even in
the most intimate moments.

'Once you asked me what I'm thinking
I lay back and think of England
Do you know the real answer?
I was born to be a dancer'

It was the land of Billy Liar, a quintessentially English Neverland where work controls you and the only way to stop it grinding you down is by coating yourself in an armour of humour and an assumption of 'removed-ness' from everyday life. It was the only way that life could be celebrated and the secret was to put as much into the celebrating as possible – something was reflected in the anthemic rushes in so many of the choruses. And this was what they had intended when they re-cast themselves as Kaisers. Humour was their secret weapon. Ricky said, 'Going "Ohhhhhhhhh" and repeating one line four times in the chorus is kinda being funny.'

Even the album title was a bit of a joke, a mocking reference to their long travails when they thought they were on the road to failure, but stayed the course nonetheless. 'We had to work a lot of shitty full time jobs to keep us going, so I suppose it's a reflection of what we've been doing over the past couple of years,' remembered Nick.

'Some of us had to work in right shithouses. Yeah, one of us used to work in a factory, one worked in a pub, and I was a DJ, just normal jobs really.' Nick, in particular, likes to send up the band's early angst-ridden slog.

He added deadpan, 'So we all packed it in when we got signed last August to do what we've always wanted to do.'

With the album ready, they looked forward to a big year.

KAISER CHIEFS

I PREDICT A RIOT

2005: The Year Of The Kaisers

The first big event of 2005 for the band was undertaking their first ever tour in America. What were the American going to make of Leeds? The Kaisers?'

It was a meticulously planned but brief trip with radio appearances, photoshoots and interviews... and a lot riding on it. The nerves started to kick well before the shows and Ricky was sick before going on stage in L.A.

But the single of 'I Predict A Riot' had been timed to roughly coincide with the trip and the Kaisers found to their amazement that it was the most requested song on the influential KROQ radio show.

'They're really into it,' Ricky told the music press back home. 'We were in a van and we were listening to "I Predict A Riot" and the DJ says "It's Kaiser Chiefs on KROQ". He said it like it was the most natural thing in the world – it's being played all the time. I can't comprehend how big that is.'

It is easy to forget how big it was. For some time now new British bands have not cut it with US audiences. Even the biggest Britpop bands that preceded the Kaisers, like Oasis and Blur, had ran into a brick wall in America. In fact, such was Blur's failure to make an impact, they all but gave up on trying to get an audience over there. What both of them lacked, of course, was a single like 'I Predict A Riot, which touched on the emotions of American youth. With bands like Green Day carrying the torch of the punk, something that was so redolent of the Clash would be bound to hit the spot.

The Kaisers were lapped up at the shows in L.A. and later, San Francisco — the crowds rocking, in particular, to Ricky's dazzling live performances.

Back in the UK, the band got back to entertaining English crowds on the **NME** Shockwaves tour, hitting the road with the likes of the Killers, the Futureheads and other indie groups. The band really enjoyed the experience of being with all the different outfits and revelled in the festive atmosphere that it inspired: 'We're like an army of bands all coming together to deliver a really good party vibe,' Ricky recounts. 'Everyone here would agree with me that we're on the best tour in the world right now.'

The tour was booked to appear in Glasgow and just before the gig Alex Kapranos, frontman of rival band Franz Ferdinand, emailed to tell them that he and Bob Hardy were coming to cheer them along and, afterwards, take them round the city. They were seen whooping it up in the audience, and Alex told the **NME**:

'What a line-up. They are amazing. And some of those lyrics... they're just genius.'

The Kaisers had just turned heads in the States of course, but this was possibly even more significant than that. It signalled that the Kaisers were now coming up alongside indie darlings Franz Ferdinand. A pivotal moment indeed.

Just as importantly, the tour was building a solid fanbase: the gigs were sold out and their reception by the fans was singalong.

They were a hit.

Franz Ferdinand
NICHOLAS ARTSRUNIK

artnik books

But this was only a build up for the **NME** awards of course, which followed a flying visit to Canada. At the awards, the band played a show-stealing set that, as Andy realised while on stage, gained them some new illustrious fans:

'I particularly enjoyed playing. I looked out from the stage and I saw Paul McCartney nodding his head and Noel Gallagher singing along.'

But the band weren't only there to play.

They were also the surprised and delighted recipients of the **NME**'s Philip Hall Radar Award. Philip Hall was the former manager of the Manic Street Preachers and a much-respected music PR guru who had died tragically young of cancer in the 90s. The award was inaugurated to recognise the 'brightest hope for the following year'. And who were the previous year's winners? Franz Ferdinand.

When they were asked how they felt, Andy and Ricky put it all in perspective, going over the last twelve months. Andy: 'The first six months were a bit boring, we were still doing jobs.'

Ricky: 'We flew in from Toronto and we're all pretty wired…when your dreams come true you just don't realise. But I'm enjoying every minute of it.'

But their biggest thrill was releasing the album. In their previous incarnation Parva, they had been ready to record an album when their record company, Mantra, folded. Peanut remembered: 'We were really skint and I was quite depressed at the time. There's lots about that period that I don't remember.' **Employment** was a symbolic release for them. And the way that the album was embraced suggested that it was also a symbolic moment for the listeners. The soundtrack to a happy ending after a long struggle (something that so many could identify with), its singalong choruses and deft mixture of frantically paced blitzes with 'slower' thoughtful stompers made it a classic of rock's DIY morality tales.

It hearkened back to the days of punk when people believed that a bit of musical skill and a lot of attitude took you a long way, but seamlessly woven into the musical cloth were nostalgic references to Britpop and great British pop acts of the past. The album magpied ideas from everyone from the Kinks and Madness to the Jam.

All in all, it was a heady brew of cheeky music that people bought in their droves.

Within a few weeks, the band had sold 325,000 copies in the UK alone.

The press coverage suggested that the critics were just as ecstatic as the fans at this finely honed fusion of the best musical traditions. **Mojo** said it 'smelts the classic rock canon (Madness, Blur, Bowie, Small Faces) into an infectious, head-spinning punch.' While **The Guardian** reported: 'That **Employment** is derivative is both undeniable and irrelevant. It is so confident, so smart, so full of life, that a more enjoyable 45 minutes is hard to imagine.'

But what was perhaps even more interesting was the reaction in the States. The Kaisers seemed to have cracked the code for success in the States by coming up with a melange of the best of British rock. Suddenly they were like a five-man band British Invasion.

KAISER CHIEFS
THE CHANGES + CANASTA

THURSDAY 24 MARCH 2005
DOUBLE DOOR + 1572 N MILWAUKEE AVE

'Old-school British-rock fans used to wear buttons proclaiming GOD SAVE THE KINKS,' wrote **Rolling Stone**. 'Now those buttons will have to read GOD SAVE THE KAISER CHIEFS! The Kaiser Chiefs make you want to sing along with practically every song by the second chorus.

'They predict a riot? They already are one.'

The **Los Angeles Times** called it a 'delirious dip into the Britpop wellspring attended by the likes of Roxy Music, Blur and Madness'; while the **New York Post** said something that was never said in a review for a British band: 'This band is the best new music-maker of the year.'

Their label, B-Unique, were also enjoying the buzz and felt that they had to get some product out to satisfy the demand for the band as pre-orders for the album started to build up. With the band's blessing, they decided to re-release 'Oh My God'.

This was another important indicator of a band's popularity. Re-releasing old singles to satisfy demand was something that previously only bands like the epochal Stone Roses had been able to do (it certainly hadn't happened with Franz Ferdinand). B-Unique's decision proved spot on as the song stormed up the charts to No six.

The reviews were phenomenal with the **NME** so keen on it, they admitted to being tempted to put it in as Track of the Week for two weeks running, and giving it another review anyway! 'A huge slice of wistful, anthemic kitchen sink drama, alternately wry and enraged, with a gigantic shoutalong finale and an almost laughable sense of poise and style.'

And on tour at the end of February the scenes were getting more and more frantic. Ricky had already gained headlines on the Shockwaves tour for his blind leaps into the audience and/or the photo pit, totally knocking the line – which he was peddling about himself – that he was 'sickly'.

And he wasn't just doing it for the big shows: he worked the stunt in at two shows in a day at record stores in Sheffield and Leeds, then at a gig in London's tiny, but celebrated venue, the Camden Barfly.

The **NME** published a picture of him there in in the middle of another trademark leap, held aloft by the crowd.

It was all an incredible build-up to **Employment** and still the enormity of it all was still sinking in. Ricky commented:

'It feels like we're caught in a bit of a pop whirlwind at the minute. At the moment we don't get any time off, but we're not complaining. We've had the last twenty years off!'

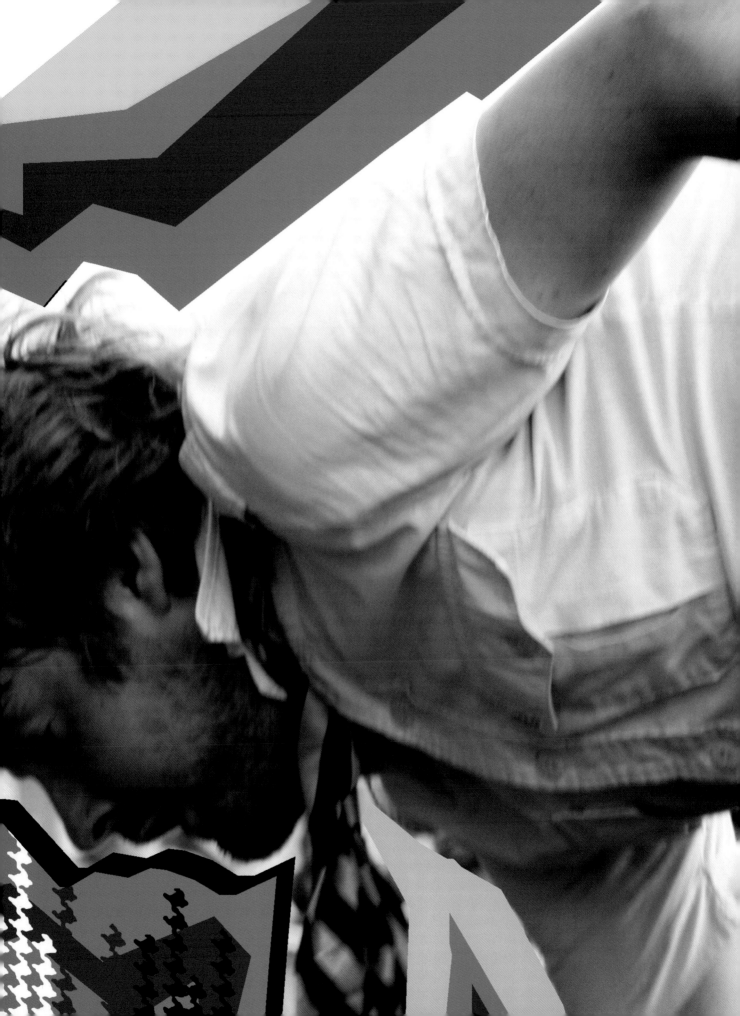

The band clearly found it hard to forget the struggle that they had had as Runston Parva and Parva. Indeed, when the Kaisers accepted the Philip Hall Radar Award, Nick couldn't resist shouting: 'Thanks for everyone who ignored us when we were Parva.'

The band had strived for years without success to play to the A&R gallery. They had confronted their own failure, then after their crisis meeting reinvented themselves as the Kaisers. Naturally they were proud of the fact that they had done it without any input from the industry, but equally understandably they were slightly bitter at the way their earlier ensembles were ignored.

In an interview in March, Nick couldn't resist telling it like it is (though in a more measured way) when he gave a fascinating insight into the way that A&R men work – and how the Kaisers had really been wasting their time.

'Over the last couple of years I have met nearly all the men (I don't think I've met an A&R woman) in the country,' he said. 'They have left quite an impression on me and the Kaiser Chiefs. So much so that when meet one now, or hear that one's about, I shudder.'

He went on to tell demoralising tales of the A&R men who pick up on the 'buzz' about a band, then swarm like flies round the honeypot: a cliquey, self-regarding circle who buy drinks and give lifts to each other, stand together at gigs, insist on being put on guest lists for gigs, but will only actually attend after they know that other A&R men will be present. 'After the gig I would go straight to the [A&R] list to see how many names had been ticked off. Sometimes one, but more often none had seen us,' said Nick.

Though he described them as 'a necessary evil', it was in the end, heartening, not demoralising to read because the Kaisers had really done it all on their own, reinventing themselves rather than fervently listening to what A&R men told them. Moreover, reports were beginning to filter out about a Sheffield band called the Arctic Monkeys who had actually barred A&R men from their guest lists whilst building up a huge audience entirely through their own gigs and via the internet.

Times were a-changin' and the Kaisers were at the cutting edge of exciting new contours in our future rock'n'roll landscape. And, like the Arctic Monkeys, they were Northern and more lyrics than musicianship.

artnik books

These were electrifying times, indeed. The press started to focus on the band and, especially Ricky, in greater depth. Even the **Daily Sta**r wanted to know what Ricky had to say about a certain singer in a band called Babyshambles.

Pete Doherty was the chief prey of the tabloid press at that time, with a prurient fascination about his liaison with Kate Moss and his drink and drug problems. It pointed to the heart of the changing landscape in music that Ricky, the sickly child who was abstaining from caffeine on tour should be asked about this renegade who was still the favourite anti-hero of many of the fans. But not to Ricky: 'He's a bit of a wally: he had the world at his fingertips and he's thrown it all away.'

It was caught by the rest of the press and when the NME finally got hold of him – on his way into Leeds on the bus, getting off at the St John's Shopping Centre and going into Harvey Nichols.

It all reflected that people were beginning to tire of rock stars in the mould of Doherty or Liam Gallagher, mouthing off and becoming part of the celebrity culture.

There was no way anyone could think of the Chiefs as celebrities, just being musicians with songs seemed to be back in vogue.

That they were in vogue was in no doubt as they graced the cover of the **NME** the next week. It served as a thank you to the **NME** for all the positive coverage that they had given the band and also a build up to the album that was nearing release. More interesting perhaps was the revelations about the attitude to the band in the early days – it was a miracle that they had ever got this far.

Their Parva days in the wilderness still came back to remind them of the unrewarded grind. When Mantra folded, it was just two days before they were due to receive the second part of an advance. They each got full-time jobs but kept on putting gigs whenever they had spare time. Ricky remembered: 'We were constantly going to London, spending £500 putting on a gig which no-one turned up to.'

But just about the time **Employment** was released, they all got demands from the Inland Revenue for back taxes. It triggered the reminiscences. Andy revealed that he had actually walked out of the band; Ricky recalled being on the receiving end of jeers at the band's failure, which cut to the quick – 'People would whisper and snigger. At one point someone came up and said "Ricky! How's your fucked-up life going?' While Nick was DJ'ing someone shouted at him, 'Oi! Boy without a record deal! Turn that shit off!'

It was a wonder that they had even stayed interested in music but a refreshing, homey attitude which wasn't too resentful (despite all the needless resentment that had been dealt out to them) marked their comments:

'I'd be the daftest man in the world if I didn't feel a little smug about how I fooled everybody into thinking it was a good idea to buy Kaiser Chiefs' records. But I'm just enjoying myself.'

He also enjoyed himself relaying his answer to one question about how his 'fucked up life was going' – 'It's up in the air, like your mum's legs.'

Following the launch of the album, the music world began to acquaint itself with the idea that the Kaiser Chiefs were going to be around for a lot longer than one album. One single on **Employment** – 'Every Day I Love You Less and Less' – was talked about in the music press as a classic. Its Morrissey-esque title suggested a Smiths song but instead of chiming guitars there were manic keyboards and instead of an gravely intoned complex lyrics, there was a raucous singalong – possibly the best 'na-na-na-na' since 'Hey Jude'.

The reception to to this song brought back some of the euphoria of a bygone era and, in some quarters, Kaisers were singled out as the leading light of 'the Britpop revival'. This was too much for an indie elder statesman who was part of the original phenomenon.

The Gallagher brothers were famously suspicious of just about any new band that turned up on the scene that they had dominated for so long and journalists would delight in baiting them with the names of any young pretenders.

Noel Gallagher had been seen singing along to one of their songs, of course, but younger brother Liam was not too happy when someone dared to bring up the name of the Kaisers in front of him.

'They're just a bad Blur,' he said. 'I'm not 'aving it. They wear make-up!'

Liam's comments was instantly relayed back to Ricky who was far from getting into a bust-up: 'I was chuffed to bits. To even occupy space in Liam's mind so he'd open his mouth about us is a compliment. He had a go at me for wearing make up, but I only ever wore make up to look more like him. It's hard to get that swarthy look in your eyes when you're a ginger.'

It was the sort of reply that could quite possibly have sent Liam scuttling along to his coke dealer to restore his morale. All of a sudden, the band had a quotable as well as a dynamic frontman.

The charm seemed to be working everywhere as the band started to gig further afield, to Europe (in a private plane) and to continue their seemingly mutual love affair with America – and this led to a more sunny encounter with Britpop legend Damon Albarn. He had been making positive noises about the Chiefs and they had all met up at the South By SouthWest Music Festival. Nick quipped to the BBC: 'We took him to see Graham Coxon!' Their set was initially 'marred' by Ricky tearing a ligament in his leg because of the venom of his performance – but it seemed to spur him on and the crowd, seeing that he had hurt himself, roared him on.

Having broke the ice in this way, it was no great surprise when Albarn joined them onstage in Toronto a couple of weeks later.

For those in the audience who were fans of both bands it must have been odd to see the elder statesman of rock alongside the frantic lead singer, whose live perform-ances did remind one of Damon Albarn in the **Parklife** era. For one onlooker it was a symbolic moment to be treasured: 'You've got to love an unscripted appearance like that. It made for a real one-off kind of experience. It was an unforgettable night.'

The next stop for them was Glastonbury. A joke about the Kaisers had been that they had always wanted to do a gig at the Leeds Festival, which given they were Leeds born and bred should have been a piece of cake – but the Festival refused to have them. Their appearance at Glastonbury was prefaced with the usual questions about what they thought of the bill this year, how does it compare to Glastonburys of the past and so on. When Nick was asked what his best 'Glasto memory' was, he promptly replied: 'Probably seeing Pulp play "Common People". Except I wasn't actually there. I've never been to Glastonbury. I always said we'd go when we played. It's taken 10 years!'

It was something that a lot of rock stars wouldn't have 'fessed to, but it added to their charm, gave them a special appeal to their growing army of fans. They were clearly as excited at playing on the same bill with the big band as the fans were to watch them. They were also pleased to be among fans who had been labouring in a very muddy Glastonbury that year.

They proceeded to wake them out of their 'mud-induced stupor' with a manic performance that was one of the highlights of the festival. Their first Glastonbury was memorable indeed and walking offstage they still had a night of excited star-watching ahead of them.

It was fitting that they should moving in such rarefied settings now because they were now in the frame for a live appearance that was going to be pretty mind-blowing. 2005 saw the twentieth anniversary of perhaps rock's greatest ever live event, Live 8. Sir Bob Geldof had been pressed for a long time about whether he would organise another event like this and, after stonewalling for a while, he came up with something on an even grander scale. Instead of concerts in the UK and US, the efforts were nearly tripled to take in five of the G8 countries whose income could make the difference between life and death to the world's poor.

The Kaisers watched with everyone else as the line-up for the UK concert was announced, with its strong representation of indie bands. Coldplay, Razorlight and Keane were all there along with the likes of Paul McCartney, Madonna and a specially reformed Pink Floyd. But they wouldn't have to feel left out – they were appearing in the American event.

For a band from Leeds, with a habit for backstage nerves, to be playing in Philadelphia with the likes of Stevie Wonder and Bon Jovi was the mother of all gigs. Needless to say, they were '*over the moon*'. Peanut likes to use the occasional bit of football-speak. He continued:

'We've done some big shows but nothing this big. You have all these bands that have done these massive shows before and they've always got covers and special extended versions of songs in the bag ready to be just pulled out of the hat. I'm thinking now – what can we do?'

The enormity of what was facing them was there in Nick's remark: 'We could call up everyone we knew in America and I still don't think it would beat P Diddy's entourage.'

And the trademark quip was ready too: 'It would be great to get 50 Cent to come and start rapping onstage with us?'

Of course, 50 Cent never happened but, if the Kaisers were totally incongruous on this bill, in the end it was a charming anomaly. In pure showbiz terms, a lot of the acts were overawed by the importance of the cause and became a little too earnest. It was even thought that the Kaisers' frantic style would lower the tone of the event. Plus it seemed like they weren't well drilled enough as a band to succeed in the slickly-choreographed setting of Live 8. But their set was actually the shot in the arm that the event needed: while the US show was deemed a bit of a disappointment, Kaisers were singled out as the exception and were praised to the skies.

The UK show was the most memorable of the five gigs and had a lot of splendid moments, but the fact that the Kaisers did it in the States (and got a fairly good reception) was definitely an eagle feather in their headdress.

They got all the recognition that they wanted when they were coming back through Heathrow and bumped into Sir Bob Geldof no less: he walked straight over and said 'Saw you on telly last night... Fucking brilliant!'

They were heading home soon enough already anyway. The route took in Dublin where they played the Oxegen festival halfway down the bill, only to storm through like the headliners. Despite the reception to the album and the singles, Live 8, Glastonbury, the **NME** award and the hobnobbing with the stars they weren't quite headliners yet, but it only suited their self-effacing, eminently 'indie' style.

Their next American tour was supporting the Foo Fighters and Dave Grohl ('the nicest man in rock') and they were brought together on the bill for an NME 'summit' at the T In The Park Festival.

When Grohl was asked who was the most famous person in his address book he was able to say Cameron Diaz. Ricky's reply? 'Er, Ryan from the Cribs.'

As for touring in the UK, they were more than happy to go on the **NME** Rock N Riot Tour in the autumn. The band was also pleased to talk up others, like the Cribs and Maximo Park, who were going along for the ride. This wasn't their first tour by any means and, even though they'd recently been sharing stages with Damon Albarn and American rock legends, they showed it hadn't gone to their heads. If anything, they were just as excited about playing with a couple of bands from the regions as they were with sharing a bill with 50 Cent. 'Northern bands are always the best anyway,' said Ricky. 'It's going to be a party, don't worry about that, and everyone can come.' That wasn't all that was exciting Ricky though:

'I really enjoyed our last tour, it was marvellous – but this one is going to be even better because we're getting catering!'

Although they were putting their typically self-deprecating spin on it, it was a tour that couldn't in all honesty meet the demand that there was to see them live. Every gig was a sell-out and a black market sprung up for tickets. The line-up was originally signed up to play the usual five dates but the demand for tickets was such that the tour organisers doubled the shows.

Ricky was getting more laconic by the minute as he commented on their popularity: 'I don't want any of my mates ringing me up and asking for guestlist. They should have tried to buy a ticket first. I don't want to have to deal with about fifty emails on the day of every gig. My mates always go, "I would have bought tickets but I didn't think it would sell out that quick!"'

The only taint on their image now was reminiscent of the bad-taste slurs that music journos used to lay on them when they were no-hopers back in Leeds. One of the fall-outs from Live 8 was the question of how bands dealt with the profitable spin-offs from this global exposure. Pink Floyd had led the way by donating to the make-poverty-history cause any returns from sales of their albums which were clearly a consequence of their Live 8 set. Not all bands followed suit and some, like Razorlight and the Kaisers, were accused of profiting from charity.

When Ricky was asked 'Are you going to give the money back?' he replied, 'What money? We haven't even paid the record company back yet.' He pointed out that they were still poor, while Pink Floyd were all mega-rich.

Their record company was also gearing up to re-release 'I Predict A Riot': this was an all too cynical exercise to some, not excused by the ploy of making it a double A side with a new song, 'Sink That Shop' alongside their anthem.

They were accused of conning the kids: 'It's not conning the kids,' said Nick. 'It's more conning the adults. The kids are all aware of where we're at.'

There was an idea in some quarters that their disregard for 'cool' was actually hiding a faux-naivete and, to their horror, they found themselves on the receiving end of bitching (probably jealous) bands again. The Kooks stuck the boot in to the Kaisers saying that they made 'soulless music and it's all about marketing'. There were also jibes about Ricky's weight (though it wasn't as if he was turning into Barry White or anything) and snide mutterings that Andy lied about his age (he hadn't, he had just moaned to the press about the ageist tendencies of A&R men).

When tackled by the **NME** on 'marketing', they kept it humourous. Peanut: said, 'Marketing? It's not like we're in the papers talking about our drug habits and then it's "Oh, by the way, we've also got an album out next week." Which we have. And it's shit.'

Ricky added, 'We've never had to slag off anyone to get in the NME. Didn't one of the Kooks go to stage school?'

Ricky's genial nature was tested yet further when he had another accident caused by his onstage antics. This was in Portugal and he tore his ligaments once more: 'I'd like to say something amazing happened like I was swinging from a lighting rig or saving a baby but no, I tripped over a mike stand onstage in Portugal. It was a bit stupid and it hurt like hell. It still does and I've run out of painkillers now. The funniest thing is that I came off stage lying in the backstage area surrounded by all these doctors and there was all these people peering at me.

'I was going "Grrraaaahhh!" in agony and I looked up and one of the faces was Dave Grohl holding a pint of Guinness. That's when I stopped screaming 'cos I thought "I can't look like a baby in front of Dave Grohl!"'

The band were due to play at the Chelmsford leg of the V Festival at the end of August, which was a couple of days after this, and as Ricky had to spend a night in hospital it looked like the gig would have to be cancelled. But Julian Casablancas of the Strokes had famously played gigs on crutches and Ricky was determined to do the same – and, in the event, it was a novel experience for the fans who could still sense the manic energy of Ricky even if he wasn't climbing all over them for a change.

The autumn tour in the US supporting the Foo Fighters came round all too quickly and there was almost a danger that they were burning themselves out now. They were lucky to have the steadying influence of Dave Grohl around and he and the band now became fast friends, sharing special moments in the backstage area.

'People say "Dave Grohl, really nice guy",' said Ricky, 'but he genuinely is the nicest guy I've met in a long time. The other night I'd gone to bed, but Nick and Simon were going to a pub across the road from the venue and it was after the Foo Fighters had played and you can imagine the pub near the venue is just full of people at the end of show, right? And Dave Grohl goes with them and just walks up and has a drink.

'And then apparently there were these two acoustic guitar guys and Dave did "Everlong" with one of the guys, and it's like the best moment of the guy's life. And then Nick, Simon and Dave played "I Predict a Riot" in this bar. Yeah, that was the wrong night to take an early night.'

In fact, the band weren't having many early nights because they were also working on new songs for the next album while they were on the tour, and they had to fly back to do a video shoot for the third and final single from **Employment**, 'The Modern Way'. This was a shoot that the band had been looking forward to doing as it had more of a personal touch than their other videos.

The band was still almost haunted by the memories of their long struggle for success and the way that they were treated, as Ricky explained to MTV. 'It's about struggling, when you know you're doing what you need to be doing, and the fact that people are just ignoring you, and the only thing you can do is just keep going and not worry about record companies. The way we did it, we just built up a big fanbase in the UK doing gigs and eventually the record companies, who all turned us down, had to notice.

'And now there's a lot of regret going around England, as far as I know, for passing on the Kaiser Chiefs, which makes me quite happy.'

Ricky had seen a live performer balancing a tennis ball on his head in Covent Garden and had fantasised about the man becoming an unlikely top TV performer through dogged perseverance, going from the street corner to street corner to having his own TV special – which the Kaisers appeared on.

In a typical Kaiser touch, the band's team actually got hold of the guy that Ricky had seen, who couldn't believe it was real when he was asked to appear on what is still their most popular video.

They tried to bring a new sense of inventiveness to the DVD format, which is now, after a band has had a hit album, an almost obligatory offering to the fans. 'People bring out live DVDs and it's a bit boring no matter how exciting the band is,' Ricky said, 'so we wanted to show some live stuff, 'cos we're a good live band. And the rest of it's made up of like silly homemade movies. It's basically just a load of weirdness, really.'

Called **Enjoyment**, it was made weirder still with the inclusion of Bill Nighy as the narrator, bringing his trademark laconic wit to the proceedings. Arguably, though, the Kaisers were funnier with their improvisations and all in all, **Enjoyment** did make for a refreshing departure from the clichéd music of the DVD genre.

By September, they had now been touring solidly for twelve months and, despite all the pressures, there were no cracks appearing in the band's make-up. As they all got on famously, there was no fissile material being made by the band's chemistry, which kinda nonplussed some of the journos who interviewed them. They get used to the tension of touring producing fireworks.

Ricky said, 'When there's five of us doing interviews abroad, they act really worried. "'Are you guys drunk?" No we're not drunk, we're just having a really good time.'

The Guardian had an in-depth piece on them, which revealed them as impossibly cheerful characters who were difficult to dislike. There must have been untold pressures on them but the closeness of the band was plain to see and, try as he might, **The Guardian** journalist couldn't even get them to admit they felt any pressure about the second album – usually dreaded after a hugely successful debut one.

The Kaisers had the perfect riposte to this: **Employment**, approaching sales of 1 million in the UK as the year was drawing to a close. The band, which had been Runston Parva and before that Parva – both equally unsuccessful – had seemed doomed before changing to Kaiser Chiefs changed their fortunes. They saw themselves as a band of cats with nine lives.

Such was their outlook that when the nominations for the Mercury Music Prize were announced and they were installed as the favourites, they let it be known that they had put a £2 bet on themselves to win. It was jokey way of seeing if they could ride their luck.

In the event, Anthony & The Johnsons walked off with the prize, which didn't faze the band. Ricky said: 'As favourites I guess us Kaiser Chiefs are easy targets, but we believe Antony's "I Am A Bird Now" record to be an accomplished piece of work and we were genuinely pleased to see him collect the award... We thought being the favourites was probably a curse.'

But they were soon to be making an even bigger splash at a much bigger awards ceremony.

2006: The Year of The Kaisers Again?

December 2005 was arguably most special for the Kaisers because they had their first days off in about a year and they were able to celebrate Christmas and the New Year in style. They had sold a million records in their home country, won **NME** awards and seemed to be breaking through in America; they had played highly acclaimed sets at Glastonbury, the V Festival (with Ricky on crutches) and one of the biggest concerts in history. It was easy to forget that they had at last played at the Leeds Festival now too – after all those years waiting, it had been completely overshadowed by these other events.

This motley crew with their ragged sense of style were now cover stars and their only UK rivals – Arctic Monkeys – were of a kind to be welcomed.

This was a band that had the balls to refuse to put the A&R men onto to the guest list at their gigs. These were not rivals: they were soul brothers whose success story was almost as unlikely as the Kaisers'.

Often unkindly called a 'band for chavs', Arctic were a group of lads, every member well under 25, who performed grimly funny, clever and aggressive songs about Sheffield skid-row in packed venues across the country. They had only been recently formed and had determined on their style and content before embarking on the road. When they did, they found instant, mushrooming success with their young fans spreading their name on the internet and causing a continuing rush of interest that almost bore comparison with Beatlemania.

The Kaisers, of course, could have been looking at an image of their younger selves if they stopped kowtowing to indie cool in their early Parva and Runston Parva days. Certainly the Arctic Monkeys were even more deprecating about rock star trappings than they were and had even turned down **Top of the Pops** because it was 'bollocks'. While the Kaisers waited for years to have their summit meeting on how to make it, Monkeys had had theirs at the very beginning of their careers. Instead of waiting for failure to lift the scales from their eyes, the Monkeys saw from the outset that the most important thing was not fitting in and being themselves.

They were a rival band to be welcomed because each of them represented a new direction in alternative music: people had grown tired of people like Pete Doherty and Liam Gallagher who appeared in the tabloids more than the music press, and for reasons that had little to do with music.

Each band were also representing the antithesis to the kind of music which – to use a choice phrase from an old Smiths song 'says nothing to me about my life'.

The press were very quick to pick up on these kinds of similarities between the two bands and always for an angle, the comparison was put to the Arctic Monkeys frontman, Alex Turner who was reported as saying: 'Most bands these days probably just write lyrics because they sound good without thinking. But I don't want to be a band like Kaiser Chiefs. I think if we're next year's Kaiser Chiefs we'll quit.'

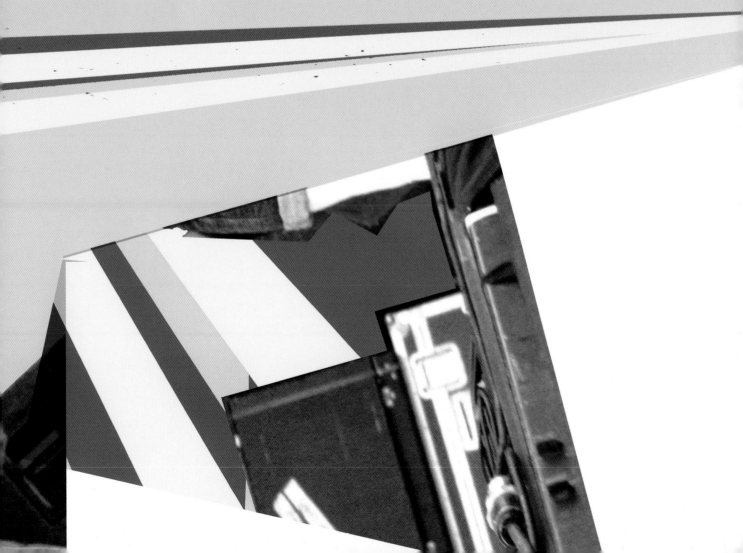

Whether or not Alex had actually listened to **Employment** is a moot point but, if the press were hoping for a retaliatory reply from the Kaisers' camp, they were to be disappointed. In fact, like a lot of people in the business, the Kaisers actually hadn't heard – because of the unique way the Monkeys had built up their fan-base – any of their records.

Nick was the first Kaiser to report back about the Sheffield group and the whole Monkeys' phenom. 'I think it's fantastic,' was his verdict. 'They are brilliant, there's no denying it.'

Eager for some new inter-band squabbling, a gutted press had to report that there had been no angry response to Turner's put-down. After years of Ian Brown feuding with John Squire, Pete Doherty robbing one friend (Carl Barat) and headbutting another (Johnny Borrell), and the Liam and Noel slagging off practically everyone, it was a refreshing dose of solidarity.

The real enemy was the rip-off music industry, not other bands, and it is the spin merchants of that industry who prime the music press to instigate these squabbles.

Kaiser were paying their dues to the real music industry – the musicians. Lead singer Tom Smith of the American indie band The Editors picked up the vibe:

'Everyone's talking about how British bands have been enjoying a great run of success recently and I think that's true. Groups like Kaiser Chiefs are brilliant.'

'Their songs are incredibly catchy. I remember seeing them at the end of last year and every song from their set was imprinted on my memory. They're one of the major success stories.'

All success is relative, of course, yet by two measures of success, the Kaiser Chiefs are still more successful than the Arctic Monkeys.

First, the Kaisers were nominated in February 2006 for no less than five Brit awards: for Best Band, Best Rock Band, Best Live Band, Best Album and Best Breakthrough Act. Booked to appear on the show as well, it was a big night for them to say the least.

They came away in triumph with no less than three of the awards – a rare feat indeed. They were rightly 'replaced' as Best Breakthrough Act by the Arctic Monkeys. But out of their three awards, the Best Live Act was most rightfully theirs as their live performances (in the face of repeated ligament damage) still had to be seen to be believed. And, of course, they capped their evening's triumph with a storming performance.

The next week, people were streaming out to buy copies of **Employment**, almost a year after it had come out.

The second measure of success was, of course, America and, significantly, their success at the Brits was heavily reported in the US media, which for years has totally disregarded British events. The Kaisers go into 2006 with a lot of goodwill in the States, which may yet end up reprising some 60s history.

The Arctic Monkeys have recreated a bit of Beatlemania in the UK, but with a bit of luck the Kaiser Chiefs could do the same thing in the US.

Vanessa Cotton whose company Triad promotes indie band in the States clarified the issue in **The Guardian**: 'Because Britain is small it's easy to be the Next Big Thing in the whole country. To tour the US, you take six months. You can do a week tour of the whole U.K. and everyone feels they're involved. People in Glasgow and Cornwall get the same national newspapers. It's unified. It's much easier building a band up over here than over there.'

All this makes sobering reading for an aspiring band but the Kaisers, with their astonishing work-rate, had already visited American several times in 2005 and are planning more visits in 2006. Americans love showmanship and this is what, as well as their music, the Kaisers have in spades. One reason they go down so well in the States is the sheer hard work they put into their act. They're are light years away from making, for instance, the mistake that Oasis did in America, when they played as statically and sullenly to US audiences as they do in the UK.

What may also help them is the resurgence of punk in the US. One of the biggest bands in the world, never mind the US, are Green Day, who have struck the proverbial chord with a huge set of disaffected youths after years of not really being taken very seriously. Their impassioned performances closely resemble those of the Kaiser Chiefs and very often one can almost see Ricky Wilson as a young Billy Joe Armstrong.

The fact that the Kaiser Chiefs are not strictly a punk band – it's just their live act that makes them feel like a punk act – also works in their favour.

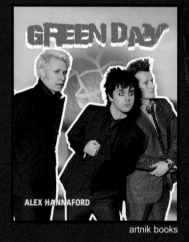

artnik books

Their clever distillation of the best of British music makes a neo-Britpop invasion of the US a tantalising possibility. If Kaiser Chiefs bring this off, it really would be an historic scalp for them. And if it doesn't happen, it's nonetheless clear that they, along with the Arctic Monkeys, will reshape the rock'n'roll landscape of the UK.

What the Kaiser Chiefs have consistently shown is a need to be true to themselves and an almost complete lack of pretension.

Whether they are enthusing about the catering on their tour, going back to Leeds to play endless homecoming/ benefit gigs or merely resisting the tiresome habit of slagging off other bands, their homespun charm and humour comes through as strongly as both qualities do in their music.

Maybe the reason they have far more fans than other cooler bands is that in their long struggle to make it they realised that sometimes it's better to be real rather than cool.

As they look forward to no doubt reaping another set of **NME** awards in 2006, they have trailered their 'second and final album' suggesting that one of them will be doing fitness videos instead. Not for them the arrogant rock star promises to dominate the world. This 'final' album is eagerly anticipated and fans can also be sure that it won't be a self-indulgent concept album or some narcissistic rock opera.

Ever since their crisis meeting in 2003, they have stuck to the simple credo of playing what they believe in, which in Ricky's words is being humorous about 'life in Leeds, and being British and young and hip'.

The Kaisers really are the ruling Chiefs of rock'n'roll.